SiReiki©: A New Journey

By Simon Clarke

SiReiki©: A New Journey text © 2018 Simon G. Clarke.

Photographs ©2018 Amanda Clarke, Simon Clarke, Iftikhar Mirza (apart from some stock images).

Contributions: Inspirations and teachers plus many others who have played a role in expanding my experiences and knowledge.

All Rights Reserved.

Dedications

A big thank you to all my teachers, family, loved ones and soul family; in any way you presented yourself to me during my journey.

A big thank you to everyone who proofed the book and gave me valuable feedback.

A big thank you to my sweet earth angel, Amanda Clarke, for your input, support, and amazing photos throughout these chapters.

Amanda is a: gifted healer, angel intuitive, artist, and my beautiful wife, who will study and grow SiReiki© with me. Namaste sweet wifey.

Photo credit Iftikhar Mirza

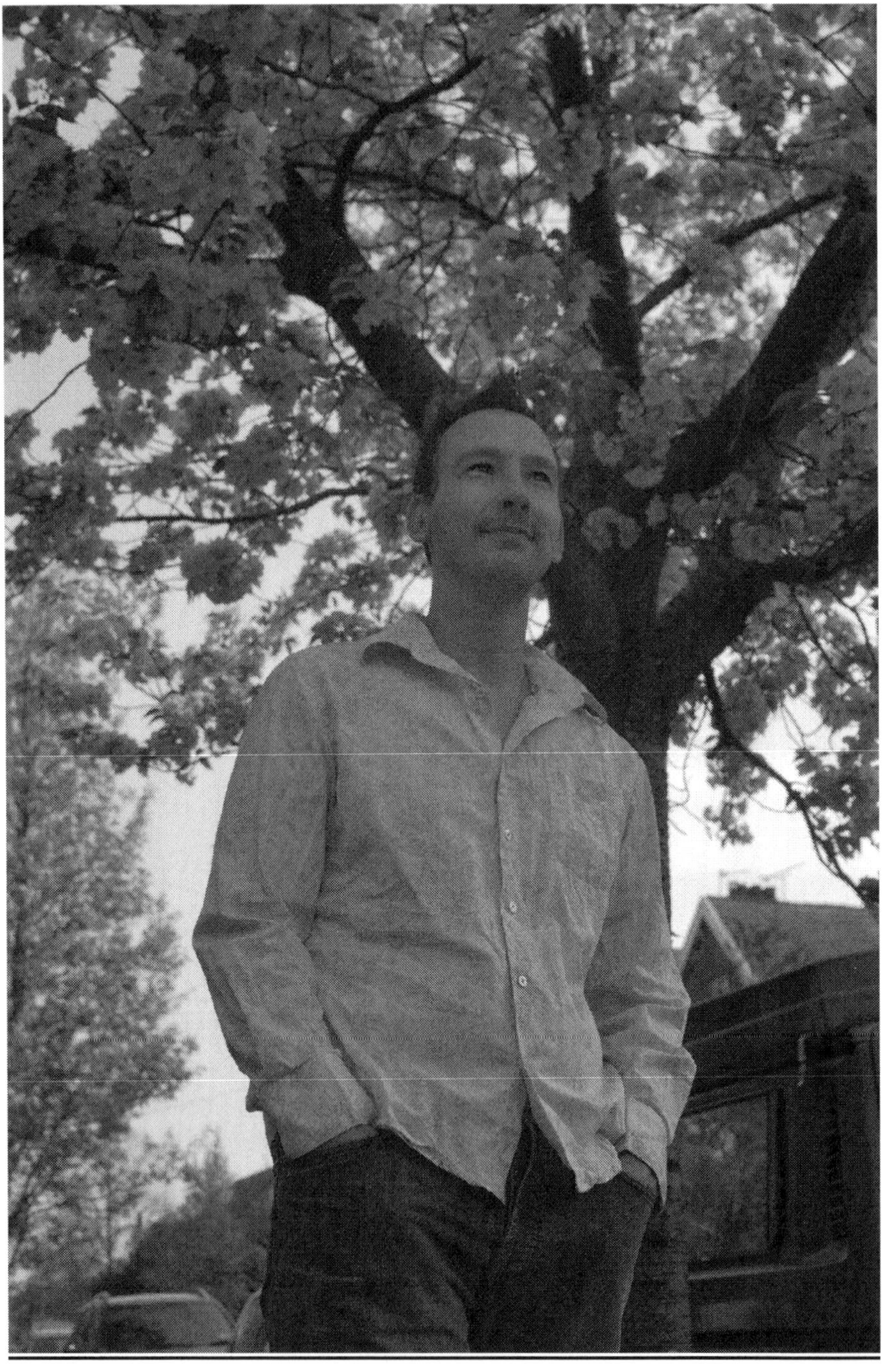

About the author:

Simon is a down to earth open-minded soul who is very passionate about Reiki. He is the first master of SiReiki and have been attuned to Usui reiki for some time. He has a background in many holistic therapies such as aromatherapy, reflexology, Indian head massage, remedial massage and have worked in the NHS as an occupational therapist. He would consider himself very spiritual though he does not follow any particular religion. Simon wishes to bring healing to those who need it by training SiReiki healers to bring this unique form of Reiki to all that are attracted to it.

Simon believes that effective complimentary therapy is something that is in anyone can grasp if you're willing to learn. Simon is happily married to a Reiki master and artist who also writes and is an intuitive.

Simon has expressed that if you wish to learn more about SiReiki or about Usui Reiki, reach out and he will make time to chat with you. Namaste love and light. Enjoy the journey.

You can connect with Simon further and let him know how you're getting on with the book with the links below:

Instagram:
@Sireiki
https://www.instagram.com/sireiki/

Reiki Brothers & Sisters of Love and Light <3 on Facebook:
https://www.facebook.com/groups/299404700398325/

Website:
https://www.sireiki.org

*The path to undiscovered joy, health and happiness starts with
a single step. A step we can all make together.*

Namaste gentle soul and welcome to my first book. It is all about the journey we take to prepare (or to reignite) for a life abundant with Reiki.

For those who have never heard of Reiki before, welcome!

This will be a new journey for you.

One I hope will change your life for the better.

I write this with hope that it is received in the intention of love, healing and awakening.

I wish to go on a journey with you to open more possibilities for Reiki do you feel like going on an adventure?

Table of Contents

Chapter 1**: **What is Reiki, Si what? And who are you Again?
Let me introduce myself. Let me show you how I see Reiki and let me share my plans for its development. For those seeking the light, hearts and minds may change. Change is on the horizon and I want to embrace it. The light will always eventually seek you. Will you come on this journey with me?

Chapter 2**: **How long is this going to take to learn? I'm kind of Busy.
This is the outline of Reiki (lightly) and exploration of SiReiki©. It's all about preparation to use Reiki in your daily practice. No, you can't learn Reiki from reading this book alone, but it's a great additional tool somewhere on your healing journey. Moreover, I want you to know what possibilities are out there in the healing world. Before you start you need to know what you're getting yourself into, right?

Chapter 3**: **Level with me, I'm curious. How do I get the best of my healing journey Again? No gimmicks, no pretence, just something to get you started. Maybe you're not attuned now or maybe you are a Usui master. We are all still learning. Consider if it resonates with you.

Chapter 4**: **You want me to eat F**G Twigs!?***
Surprise! Change is coming! Are you open enough to embrace it?

Chapter 5: Ohmmmm a start to your Learning
A start to your studies, we all have to start somewhere in our healing journey. Here are a few points to think about to prepare you for the last stage – The Attunement. If you flow the steps your learning journey will be fun, enjoyable and smooth.

Chapter 1
What is Reiki, Si what? Who are you again?

The word Reiki is made of two Japanese words - **Rei** which means "God's or Source's wisdom", or "the Higher Power or higher mind" and **Ki** which is "universal life force energy".

Rei, when translated, can mean the words God, universe, or higher mind. It refers to the aspect of Reiki that guides the universal life energy while also referring to its infinite source.

In a way, it means all three definitions. I know it's a little vague, but it is a Japanese translation and it has room for interpretation as the meanings are interlinked.

Ki, is an easier concept one that is understood by most. It is the life force that flows in all living beings. When our Ki is blocked or depleted from a healthy flow, our health is negatively affected. A healthy flow of Ki will nourish the physical body, promote healing, balance and wellbeing.

To westernize the concept of Reiki, simply think of Reiki as an oxygen tank or as a natural nutritious, healing food. Burn victims are placed in oxygen tanks to promote healing of tissue as the body heals itself. This is the effect of having super oxygenated cells via the pure oxygen intake. We need oxygen and nutrition to function. Without adequate levels, our tissue will die. Moreover, when optimum levels of nutrition and oxygen enter our body, it is capable of profound facilitated healing very quickly.

Your body is made of energy, and your being expands farther than the reaches of your skin. Your thoughts and emotions directly affect the energy within you. Your tissue and organs are simply blocks of energy in physical form. For this understanding, you need to only look at the structure of an atom.

By working on the energy systems via the introduction of Reiki, you remove blockages and disturbances in Ki flow. This has direct effect on the emotional and physical body. While instructing the body to maintain itself in a particular way, it is comparable to the introduction of nutritious food or medicine with no side effects; fueling tissue repair of the physical body.

In its simplest concepts, Reiki is not that difficult to break down into familiar aspects. You must accept Reiki with your own personal comfort level. It is simultaneously very simple and highly complex. Your viewpoint will likely change with your experiences as a Reiki practitioner, so just keep an open mind and respect other's beliefs.

Reiki is a thing of wonder, and in a way I still feel that my awareness of Reiki will continue to grow long after I have developed my system and integrated this into my teachings. I believe my students will further expand the system, so advanced developments and alterations can be possible. With that, other forms of Reiki certainly will be developed.

*My name is Simon. I am a 36-year-old Reiki master and creator of **SiReiki©**. I started to learn healing art forms in 1999 as I was motivated to help myself and others.*

I have always had a strong drive to help others. Especially those I care about who struggle with health problems. Reiki is a very useful tool and through it you will help yourself and others.

I believe that as humans, we require a little help in ways that compliment healing of the whole person, rather than just a symptom of the illness.

This led me to learn holistic therapy (which I studied for 2 years). I worked for various spas, also on a cruise ship internationally. However, due to a few physical faults, I was not suited to remedial massage. Leaving the cruise ships with Repetitive Strain Injury (RSI) in a few areas, my confidence was shaken.

During my holistic training, prior to leaving the ships, I started my Reiki journey and met my first master. With my first master I trained to a level 2 practitioner I learnt a lot from her and have a lot of respect for her. Reiki soon became a precious gift that I would always utilise.

Reiki helped me come out of the cycle of pain medication that I had had since childhood. It was key to grow my emotional intelligence, wellbeing, and spirituality. I kept my hand in Reiki and introduced many people to the system while I was working internationally on the cruise ships. Still, I found it difficult to start out as a Reiki practitioner in my home town without a suitable base of my own. I thought to myself that I needed further training as my holistic therapies were not fully supporting me. I moved on to study sport science and mainstream health in order to bring my love of helping people to the forefront.

I knew that the Reiki would always be a big part of my life. Over time I continued my Reiki practice and became a master. At the same time, I worked on charitable Reiki when I could, by making a small difference when possible in my own way.

Since 2007, I wanted to start a new system of Reiki; one that I could enhance with guidance given to me and knowledge acquired.

I spoke in depth with my new master about it several times, but I went through some difficulties that put that on hold for a while. We all face challenges in our journey.

We must continue to move along our path and be aware of all the important lessons we come across along the way. Moving forward to 2016, I started working on my system.
Even with the majority completed, I am still working on it, continuing to evolve through personal growth and teaching.

This is the not the finish line.
This is a new start in my journey of ***healing****.*

I wish to share my gifts with the world, I'm not important...

But my message could well be for some.
My techniques could be utilised to help many. That is my wish.

My system is designed and guided to enhance traditional Reiki.

The marriage of tried and tested knowledge brought together with channelled guidance to enhance an already near perfect system.

If you are curious or have decided you would want to learn Reiki, then this book is for you. Think of it as a pre-attunement manual from my standpoint and a little introduction to my form of Reiki that I am developing, "SiReiki©".

It does not matter if you believe in all as I do... just keep an open mind and use what resonates with you.

If you already practice Reiki, this system may enhance your practice even without an attunement, but you won't get the full benefit without it.

If you don't practice Reiki, my writings, my teachings will open your eyes to unseen possibilities that may spark an interest. After you finish reading, you can decide if what you read does or does not resonate with you. There is an abundance of systems that branch off of the Usui core, though I see SiReiki© as unique and valued.

You may prefer a different technique or teacher and that is the natural way of things. If anything, I hope by reading this, you gain a respect for Reiki in all its forms. If you are so guided, I will teach you mine.

Happy reading. Take your time.

It's not a race! So work at your own pace.

Unlike other forms of Reiki, SiReiki© changes a lot around the client's preferences, and uses the practitioner's knowledge of holistic therapies to aid the healing process. Rather than bringing a set template of rigidity to the table, each session can be slightly different with no two SiReiki© sessions being the same.

I am getting ahead of myself. This book is not about learning SiReiki©, but acts as an additional reference while you're on your Usui Reiki journey. It introduces my healing system as something to think about for the future.

So don't be confused, you don't have to learn SiReiki© to get benefits from my teachings or even Usui Reiki for that matter. It's simply a guide to my viewpoint of Reiki, with a manual for how to prepare for a life rich with Reiki.

Usui Reiki is the core system of healing which other forms have been developed from, so your journey starts with the Usui Core. Instead of repeating instructions for a well-defined Usui system, I wish to share my viewpoints and act as one author who may help to shape your Reiki Journey. I simply wish to introduce Reiki in my own way, from my perspective. This guidance is just as important at the very start as it is at the end of your Usui journey. It is my intention that this book will act as a starting point just as much as a restart point in your Reiki journey.

What is Reiki and how can I use it to benefit myself and others? Reiki can be depicted as: "**spiritually guided universal life force energy**". Reiki is a healing art and a spiritual practice that does not require religious belief or special powers. You can incorporate your beliefs. Reiki will not take you off of a religious path if you indeed are on one. Instead, it will deepen your spirituality. Reiki is a method of bringing about **balance, peace, health and wellbeing** in all forms.

It has enriched my life and changed how I interact with the **world**. Reiki is my core. It is like a compass in my life, not just a healing tool. It is much more.

If you go fully into Reiki, your life won't be the same again. When you look back, it will be with great appreciation. You will be thankful for it and those in your life will also be thankful, as I'm sure you will touch many lives. Namaste

In its intended forms, Reiki is a transformation to a higher alignment of being, a new way of life. In my vision for Reiki, veganism, ethics and spirituality are all central.

If you practice Reiki but don't live an ethical life, you are not getting the best out of your journey. An ethical life is spiritual by nature, but with Reiki, you are aware the energy is guided. This energy comes from not from you, but by a source where it came from. Spirituality is not a requirement. It is a defining element in all forms of Reiki. You take from it what you will.

Reiki was discovered through study and mediation by Master Mikao Usui. He discovered the Reiki system and passed it on, helping many people. He was a great man and teacher. Reiki spread from East to West and now is a worldwide system. Thanks to him and those in his lineage, Reiki now has a strong reputation. Many believe Reiki predates this discovery, which it clearly does. However, this is the pivotal version now in use by most Reiki practitioners.

Namaste teachers.

May your spirit shine brightly with light.

Reiki is extremely relaxing 99% of the time. It feels like **sunbathing** on a nice beach as a gentle warmth moves through you. You relax into a state of peace. Your body relaxes but your spirit and your consciousness is awakened. It is common for clients to enter REM sleep while an aspect of the mind can remain lightly awake. Those who need sleep, will fall into a pleasant full sleep. It calms anxiety, it reduces or removes pain, and it reduces negative emotions and eases painful experiences. It promotes healing and programs the body to heal itself at a highly increased rate. It can reduce or remove the side effects of mainstream medicine, even considered an effective treatment in its own right independently.

Reiki can be administered with or without clothing, in person touching, or a few feet away, or even anywhere else on earth distantly. It has no contraindications, is safe for any age and will reinforce mainstream treatment, working in tandem with it. Reiki removes negative energy and pollutions from your energy field and removes energetic blockages. It works holistically to promote health and wellbeing.

A simplified viewpoint would be that a little, often, helps, and a lot makes a big impact. If you are in good health, your sense of wellbeing will be amplified. You can notice a benefit for even a 15-minute session for some relief, but for best effect allow 60 minutes.

If you are in a medical setting (I'm mostly talking to my American readers but it can apply elsewhere as appropriate) regular shorter sessions would be a cost effective alternative to full hour sessions. As an allied health professional, I see application potential for Reiki worldwide, working in tandem with modern Western techniques.

I wrote a paper about the topic while at university. You can read this paper by going to my blog: https: sireiki.org. It's not definitive work, but in order to be accepted as an academic piece of work, my arguments and evidence had to be valid and reliable. It is an interesting read, as is my blog in general, for those who have never explored some of the many benefits of Reiki.

The foundry evidence for the therapeutic nature of Reiki exists. Moreover, application within the National Health Service (NHS) here in the United Kingdom (UK) could be affordable (even money saving) and easy to administer. Current research on the efficacy of Reiki is available if you search for it online, but the funding is not always there to study it in a variety of clinical settings. A number of the studies come from outside the UK, so do some looking around. The trick is to gain what knowledge you can from a paper while being aware of its limitations, rather than seeing one, or a few papers, as a definitive guide. One misconception with studies has been a lack of explanatory theory. You can measure the effects of Reiki (sometimes only subjectively but it is always measurable), but the full understanding of Reiki's concepts is in its infancy.

Ancient knowledge takes a lot of scientific understanding to explain. That does not mean that such knowledge is beyond us. We have only just begun to seek out such knowledge. For some, Reiki is too much of a leap of faith and do not see it as appropriate in the medical field. Some of the underpinning science of Reiki is only just beginning to be understood, is only accessed by a few, or is not currently available.

Progress has been made in the field of energy and vibrational science. Some of the scientific community's application will not be possible without full understanding. Not fully understanding commonly found medicines such as Paracetamol (used to treat minor pain, fever; often known as Tylenol), did not stop its full utilisation.

The same should be applied to Reiki. It has been proven to be so far a much safer option by any comparison, so why not?

In academic circles, certain aspects of Reiki are seen as false science, such as distance Reiki. Other aspects are recognised - It is the same system, so if it works at all, it works in its entirety. In most studies, distance Reiki is not seen as valid at all and is even given as a placebo. You may read studies which find distance Reiki just as effective, and in some cases more effective, than in person sessions.

Unfortunately, the study evidence is often lagging behind findings in actual practice, and this disconnect often yields opposition from the scientific community. It will take a while until the research catches up with what Reiki practitioners have full grasp of; in common practice across the world. Result interpretation can be viewed differently, depending upon your belief in the science of distance Reiki. Don't take my word for it. Look around, especially for testimonials from actual practitioners who perform distance Reiki and their clients who have benefited from the experience.

Reiki's reputation speaks for itself. It can be very effective. I have seen this in practice. Moreover, I have read quite a few academic papers in which findings could be applied to most settings. One general theme I have found is that Reiki is usually proven to be therapeutic. It is not always found conclusively effective, but we need more data. This is mainly due to study limitations or flaws in design or understanding of background theory. In most settings, the results seem encouraging with considerable, sometimes sustained improvements.

In other studies, Reiki is only found to be slightly more effective than blind placebo. Some of these studies are designed to fight the progression to full acceptance or just are designed incorrectly.

One thing you must consider with the findings that are only slightly more effective than placebo is this – The placebo effect is often found to reduce said symptoms and has been proven to be somewhat effective.

As you think you are receiving treatment, a chain of impulses, hormones and energy direct a recovery effect that starts as purely psychological. It is scientifically recognized that some are subjectable to an improvement from the placebo effect, so by stating it was as effective as placebo is misleading.

The design of the study is key. If it's flawed from the start, the results are less valued. Unfortunately, there are those out there who don't want to see Reiki accepted by the community.

While some don't have a grasp of Reiki to correctly design the study, Reiki has had a slow acceptance so we are still developing how we design studies. Others fight the good fight, sometimes risking their reputation to prove Reiki has so much worth and potential. It's up to you to judge each source of information as something that should be criticised. There are official tools used to academically review papers. You can be as serious as you like while reviewing available research.

Don't just scan the summary of a paper. Look closely at the design, the results, the methodology and discussion (read the entire paper more than once). At first glance, the study may seem like Reiki was non-effective; this could be true. But if you look closely, you will often find that the study was not correctly designed. Learn from these studies and perhaps you will find something that can be useful to you in your exploration of Reiki.

Understanding the methodology of the study is important to interpret the results. Interpretation of journal results can be difficult unless there are clear, staggering results. My tip is look at the sample size and see how they controlled and carried out the study.

Another area to look out for is who is funding the study and is it biased? There is bias in both directions, so really think! Can the results be trusted and what did they do to eliminate bias? Validity is another area to consider. Did the study measure what it set out to prove or was it created to elicit a specific perspective?

Reliability is another issue. If the study was repeated, would the result be the same? What is the training level of the therapist, have the clients had Reiki before? What type of Reiki is utilized and will the client group find it difficult to actively receive Reiki? These are all questions you must ask yourself when seeking scientific validation of the potential application of Reiki.

A modest research fund usually means modestly small sample sizes. So trends are your friends. If a collection of well-written research that are similar, come up with similar results, the end conclusion has a stronger scientific basis.

From my understanding and personal experience, I see potential application. Reiki may not reverse disease in an instant but still has significant potential application for treatment.
It assists in recovery from addictions, emotional imbalance, pain management, stress and anxiety relief. Reiki can also assist one with anger management and promotion of relaxation. While Reiki often reduces recovery time from trauma or infection and helps to alleviate disease, it is a valid secondary tool. It will always work towards a person's greatest good.

One misunderstanding that comes across because of the way Reiki functions is that it will always do what the client wants it to do or the therapist wants it to do, this is incorrect.

Healing occurs on a priority level. The energy knows where it is needed and will go there from wherever you start the healing.

What needs to be worked on first will be worked on. This requires understanding. What needs to be worked on first, may not be what the clients have in their mind as priority; hence, this should be explained in goal setting with the client.

Though useful in understanding where a client is at that moment, through subtle cues and interpretation of an expert therapist, Reiki is never a medical diagnostic tool and should not be used in this way. Reiki is not always the appropriate pathway at that time. We must be aware of limitations and collaborate with modern techniques. Together we see the whole picture, so let's attack ill health from every side.

The chances are Reiki could be successfully utilized with most patients to enhance their already solid care.

With Reiki you can teach the client coping mechanisms for maintenance of many conditions for their entire life, or simply apply Reiki as part of their mainstream care. The majority of cost is simply time.

As far as value for money is concerned, Reiki is about as cost effective a treatment as one could possibly imagine.

I'm not saying band 5 (fully qualified degree level) and above therapists should be spending hours per day giving Reiki. That would not be cost effective. A small number of selectively trained therapists could oversee band 2, 3 and 4 (sub-degree) staff that could incorporate Reiki into a client's package of care as they see appropriate.

Level 1 Usui Reiki is very simplistic. Once taught, the client can use as needed for the rest of their lives.

This could reduce the client and health system's financial burdens. But how could Reiki save a health system money, while increasing the quality of care? It is simple.

Reiki requires minimal expense to train therapists with minimal training time. Only a very small number of experienced therapists are required. Reiki has no cost to administer at all and you don't even have to be in the client's vicinity to perform it.

While more trained staff could highlight the need for sessions and teach clients, a minimalistic model of Reiki (level 1 and 2) could teach caregivers. If, for instance, Reiki became popular within a health system and it did not want to pay for this expense of teaching the client, the service could be listed as available for a fee and encounters would be privately funded by the patient.

The cost is small and can be reduced by teaching small groups at a time with level 1. Traditionally, Reiki can be taught in approximately 4-5 hours. This time could be reduced to 2-3 hours to increase cost effectiveness.

The research is developing and promising. The value for money and ease of use is evident, but until Reiki is an approved tool recognized by the medical community, its potential to assist in many people's recovery won't be utilized and that saddens me deeply.

I say the argument for the recognition of Reiki as a valid tool for healing is vital.

The academic conflict is tiresome and needs resolution. There is plenty of evidence to come up with a general consensus on possible graded application. Professionals and researchers are split in their schools of thought and simply will not agree. In absence of this consensus there is at least, without a shadow of a doubt, justification for definitive research. Especially if it can be applied, where appropriate, to enhance care.
Reiki may never become an active part of our mainstream health care system within my lifetime but I remain hopeful that it will. Reiki may be too whimsical or magical to some, but so were many methods before they were understood adequately.

Don't misunderstand me, I will always be in awe of Reiki but I see it as just another form of medicine. Of course, Reiki is not and should not be the first point of response medically to an acute problem. Yet, its application could benefit most patients' recovery journey when it's the right time.

Bringing much-needed holism to a treatment, Reiki could be used secondarily to greatly benefit primary treatment and reduce medication dependence. While increasing wellbeing and quality of life, giving power back to the client in a person-centred way, they can continue to utilize these skills years after initial treatment. Reiki falls under the umbrella of energy or vibrational medicine. There has been much advancement within the science in recent years, but we are still some distance away from understanding it fully from a wholly scientific standpoint. We can theorize and understand many more aspects of how Reiki works than before, and can quantify readings measured during healing sessions along with subjective data from client's self-reported health.

Reiki can be compared to a prescribed medication. One dose can do a lot and sometimes is enough to cure. More often than not, multiple dosages are required and a top up dose may be required if you aggravate your complaint. That is why, for chronic conditions, the teaching pathway comes into its own. The frequency that one needs to top up the Reiki session varies from several hours to a few weeks. With more intensive illness or imbalances requiring a greater duration and frequency of Reiki intervention.

An example of limitations and applications of Reiki can be seen from an example of myself dropping a heavy glass on my foot. Excuse my simplistic analogy! My foot hurts where the glass impacted and starts to bruise, there is no open wound but I can't effectively weight bare. I administer Reiki, the pain significantly reduces or leaves completely and I can walk gently on it for a few moments without pain (with no obvious sign of fracture).

I refuse to rest to allow my body to recover, so the pain returns to protect my injured foot, now requiring additional healing and rest to eliminate the pain stimulus. I rest as directed by my doctor, and use Reiki for a smooth and prompt recovery. Before I know it, my foot is good as new and it no longer impacts my occupational function.

Reiki is a healing technique that can be achieved by most. It does not make you immune to ill health or injury or reverse all the damage incurred in one single session. It simply works with the body to bring about restoration of health and balance within limitations of the body's triggered and facilitated natural healing. Working in harmony with the body, instead of overriding the pain response, Reiki turns it down or off.

The pain response is a basic protection mechanism. Reiki works to the greater good so the pain response will return, if it is needed to protect the receiver from harm. It could be argued that Reiki is a more synergistic, holistic pain management than painkillers. Reiki, unlike strong painkillers, will not increase any risk factors for further injury. There are no side effects, only healing actions. Overdose is impossible.

Now let's say it was a larger, heavier item that I dropped onto my foot. I administer Reiki and the pain reduces but comes back when I try to walk. I go for an x-ray and my foot is fractured badly. My recovery is gradual and I need to immobilize my foot and have a minor operation. Then later I re-strengthen my foot and use a mobility aid for a short period. I help to compliment my recovery through pain relief and healing promotion with Reiki as well as mainstream intervention from a physio and possibly an occupational therapist. As I'm receiving Reiki, my pain will be much better controlled, therefore I require much less analgesic or none at all depending on how much I stick to my treatment plan for self-healing.

My stress and anxiety would be better controlled, while my autonomy remains intact as administration can be done anywhere, at any time I choose. My recovery will be quicker than mean populous as my body's facilitated healing will speed up recovery time. In addition to gaining greater advancements through rehabilitation as my pain levels are well controlled, the therapist can push me harder, reducing therapy demand, waiting times and recovery cost.

If I were to create a valid research study, it would likely find that a patient with access to Reiki will have more benefits and a smoother recovery when contrasted to those who receive the same treatment without. Moreover, it could secondarily highlight less failed discharges and potential reduction in overall cost of care.

With that in mind, the advantages of utilizing Reiki therapy and teaching by existing staff as I've discussed, are simple when it is used appropriately. The two schools of thought make up one whole; complimenting each other. When the appropriate pathway, tool or professional is used at the appropriate time, neither school of thought is neglected and requires no additional staff.

It is the word "heal" that is one reason why healing techniques have not been fully embraced by the majority of people.

To heal is not commonly an instant effect; even if symptoms can be reduced or eliminated very quickly. It is the restoration process back towards health and balance in all forms. Therefore, we must shed our miraculous view of healing, and update our understanding of Reiki as energy medicine. Profound healing can occur within a very short amount of time, but even though the source of Reiki is infinite, its effectiveness is not.

The client needs no special belief or expectation for healing to occur, but they must consent to receive. It does not happen a lot, but some clients simply don't accept the energy so the session has zero effectiveness in that case.

Reiki is a therapy in art form. It may have a spiritual core with scientific and ethical principles, but in essence, it is a universal healing tool a universal medicine. If Reiki was gradually accepted into mainstream health, we could see the original system having most suitability, and be a most logical starting point. Simple at its core, designed so that anyone can learn healing for themselves and others, the Usui system requires no previous training.

Reiki is not dependent on intelligence or complex knowledge of anatomy. Instead, it is powered by a genuine will to heal, empathy and unconditional positive regard.

These are areas of development that even my mainstream training as an occupational therapist highlighted as essential.

If you are not the most caring of people, the practice of Reiki itself will promote such qualities and will enrich your spiritual life. Reiki is taught via teachings and energy attunement. Think of it as adjusting the frequency of your bio-electrical field and pathways, so that you can channel an unlimited supply of universal life energy.

Reiki is self-guided. It knows what to do, but at the same time, specific energies are activated through the desire and activation of the Reiki practitioner. The greater your desire to help and the openness of the client, the more effective the Reiki session.

If you have never received a Reiki session, I recommend you try it at least once or twice to see how you react. Reiki as I know it is inexpensive and sometimes charitable, respecting the need for the client's healing first and foremost over financial gain.

A healer's time is highly valued and an exchange should always happen to keep things fair. Well it's more than that really. If we don't value something, it holds no significance or relevance, so the healer is wasting their time and yours.

While there are some therapists driven by ego, a true Reiki master is humble and down to earth. To practice Reiki is a privilege. As therapists, we deserve a fair exchange, but no more than any other service profession. Remember, the more your desire to heal comes from a genuine place, the more efficient a therapist you will become. That genuine will to heal will not happen if the therapist's time is not valued. I sometimes offer free healing, but it should never be expected. You would expect your doctor to treat you while not being paid for his or her time, so why do healers get called to heal for free just because we are spiritual and are supposed to be working for the greater good? #we've got to eat too.

I claim no supremacy over Reiki teachers. I am just spreading one system of naturally evolved Reiki like so many have done before.

If you want to learn Reiki from me and you're not already a student, feel free to reach out to me and I will do my best to get back to everyone as soon as I can. Go to www.sireiki.org and we can go from there.

I have a career in mainstream health which began in January 2017, in addition to my Reiki practice. I am allowing myself to settle into my new role so this book will be coming to you a little bit later that I had planned while I find my feet. Hopefully, it will be worth the wait while I work on finishing this stage of my Reiki journey. This does not mean I am stepping away from my Reiki path. Reiki will always be my center, but I'm having my cake and eating it too. This is an evolving goal as healing is healing, however it is done. It should not matter as long as you are making a difference in your world. Although there are no current plans to involve my Reiki healing activities within the scope of my NHS career, you never know when those who lead these clinical institutions may see or understand the appropriateness of integrating Reiki into mainstream healthcare pathways. With this plan in mind, I will have two callings and hopefully two ways to help people who need it.

Even though the two worlds of thinking are different, my training in Western health has influenced the development of SiReiki© and changed how I teach it. My teaching as a Reiki practitioner has influenced my job as an allied health professional. I think Reiki is an asset to modern healthcare with all grades of professionals able to grasp and utilize it. I think it is only a matter of time when it will become de-stigmatized and accepted.

Reiki utilization would likely result in client satisfaction increasing, quality of life would increase, while the cost of application is minimal and would likely cut overall healthcare expenditures. This would be a savings of tax payer's money, not another bottomless investment.

For staff, it is also a win-win. Job satisfaction would, for many, increase while sick rates would likely decline. The duration needed for recovery for sick or injured staff would also decrease. As a nice side effect, the nurturing nature of having Reiki available to staff in need would increase, as well as likely having declining rates for time off for stress related illness. This makes Reiki a money saver in every aspect rather than a financial drain.

The worlds are different on the surface. One day, the potential benefits will outweigh gaps in acceptance. The line between complementary and mainstream therapy will ever so slightly blur and the patients will greatly benefit. If, within my lifetime, I witnessed Reiki utilized by more than just rare areas of care in a hospital, I would tick off a serious life goal of my bucket list. Well, I can dream!

I think for some, SiReiki© may be a jump too far for widespread acceptance, especially within mainstream health care. That is perfectly fine as is. I have no wish to introduce my form of Reiki to this area. Usui Reiki would be suitable, but SiReiki© is too far a step into the spiritual for the mainstream. Only you will know if you are ready for the journey forward into SiReiki©.

Okay, I'm going to be straight to the point with you. I love Reiki. It is the best holistic therapy I have ever used. I always knew I could develop it if I was guided and could add a little of my earthly knowledge to it as well. I have been guided, so here it is - all singing, all dancing SiReiki©.

Basically, it is a system expanding on traditional Reiki with other frames of reference. These points were given to me that I know work. This is an ever expanding list:

- Expanded principles and various exercises for development.
- Use of affirmations and prayers.
- Expanded use of enhanced visualization, meditation and correct breathing.
- Developed grounding and protection techniques.
- Utilising angels and other helpers of the light.
- Amplifying empathy and love to enhance energy flow.
- Crystal healing and enhancements.
- Combining the benefits of massage with Reiki simultaneously.
- Aromatherapy to enhance and reinforce.
- Correct nutrition.
- Earth preservation and animal harm reduction.
- Music & sound healing.
- Group and world healing and much more.

The entire shift of technique and frequency has been graded into three levels and should take 1-2 years to master once you become a Usui Reiki master practitioner.

To use all the practices does require some additional training. Use what you're qualified for while you add to your available techniques down the line.

You might not utilise it all. There is a great deal of flexibility within the SiReiki© system. It is an adaptive system with the client at the core, allowing you to use selective elements of techniques for that client. Some techniques may not resonate with you for that individual client or for your own healing. That is how it has been designed – you can use what you are guided to for that client. It is not necessarily complex, but does require more engagement from the practitioner. A quick conversation and log of contraindications and preferences is enough to give you the starting point you need to select any additional techniques.

SiReiki© requires further training than may be considered practical in traditional Reiki. For those who already master Usui Reiki and know its benefits but want to wander further down the road of discovery, you are my intended student for this system.

As you read my teachings, your knowledge of SiReiki© will progress. Use what resonates with you and your client at that time. That is how I have designed this system to allow for fluidity rather than set out your healing tools in stone.

I am sharing this journey with you together alongside our angels and guides.
I have designed (and continue to evolve) this system as I receive and create SiReiki©.

My writings flow freely, continuously; so much so that. I am eager to teach what I have learnt.

I know it can help others as it has helped me.

Compassion has made me a strong healer.

Adversity has been a powerful teacher. As such, learning was sometimes very painful...

Some of the trials I have endured, to get me where I am today, I would not wish on my worst enemy. Through adversity and challenge, I have learned empathy and gained strength through gentleness.

There is another way to peace that is easier than suffering. I will gladly teach you what I can.

Namaste.

Photo credit Amanda Clarke

Enjoy the journey.

Take your time. It's worth it.

Chapter 2
How long is this going to take to learn? I'm kind of busy.

Usui Reiki is the grounding to SiReiki©. It is an amazing system that is simple and fun to use and so very useful, not only in professional but personal and spiritual life...

Usui Reiki

Typically, traditional Level 1 - 3 Usui Reiki Total training time is 1 -4 years+ (but no rush). Understanding the components of each level is essential to moving forward in your journey to SiReiki©. Here I share my training program used to help students achieve each level.

Usui Reiki Level 1:
Directed preparation for first attunement.
- History of Reiki & Reiki principles.
- Level 1 attunement and training half day for self-healing.
- Meet your guides meditation.
- Case study (2 people) with email and blog support.
- Level 1 manual (printed).
- 1-hour recap and case study review followed by certification.
- Average UK Price £90 for this Level.

Usui Reiki Level 2:
Level 2 Attunement and 1 full day's training for professional level Reiki.
- Using crystals with Reiki (including crystal gift).
- Intro into Reiki meditation.
- Developed grounding and protection.
- Distant and emotional healing.
- Increased healing frequency.
- Case study (3 people).
- Email, blog and live chat support.
- Level 2 manual (printed).
- Two-hour recap and case study review, followed by certification.

- Average UK Price £125 for this Level.

Usui Reiki Master Practitioner:
Master Practitioner attunements and one day's training.
- Developed Crystal usage.
- Full Reiki meditation.
- Increased healing frequency and master symbol.
- Awareness of your angels and meditation.
- Healing attunements (for other Reiki Practitioners)
- Case study (5 people).
- Full manual (printed).
- Full live chat support.
- Half a day's recap after case study. Review and certification.
- Average UK Price £350 for this Level.

Usui Reiki Master Teacher
This is a continuation from Master Practitioner level. It teaches you how to pass on the Reiki system including giving attunements.
- One to one guided teaching depending on your strengths and weakness within the system.
- With full digital manuals, tips and techniques involved in teaching.
- Full online support.
- Two client case study (Student).
- A short recap discussion and case study review, followed by certification.
- Average Price £350.

Once you have completed Usui training, you can carry on your journey with SiReiki©. It is true to the original system, while at the same time, being something unique to my teachings.

SiReiki© is my version of the continuation and progression of traditional Reiki. It will enhance your abilities and give you new tools to healing. Enjoy it as my gift to you.

SiReiki © in its broadest sense, is the practice of using Reiki in a developed way; with additional holistic therapy techniques that have been brought together in a way that's aligned to Reiki.

In essence you work with the Reiki with additional techniques to maximise effectiveness and reinforce treatment.

Adjunct Training

Aromatherapy and crystal healing are utilised in SiReiki© and require training depending upon where you practice. Even though you may not be required by law to obtain additional crystal healing certification to incorporate them in practice, some additional training will be rewarding. Universally, massage and aromatherapy require basic certification before you can practice on a client *(Always refer to local and national regulations for clinical providers before advertising services. Requirements differ by country, or level of experience).*

Massage and aromatherapy, though important, are not essential for practice. See these as additional tools that complement the SiReiki© system. If you don't have qualifications, you can still use these tools on yourself and family members. The manuals will give you a good base to start your study in this area. When you're ready to use these tools on clients, you can seek out additional training.

If you are an experienced practitioner in another holistic therapy that I don't cover; then we can work together to see how to incorporate it into your SiReiki training.
The possibilities are truly endless. Best of all your training in holistic therapies can be utilised within SiReiki. This is something I am very excited about, as I could train therapists that would give unique sessions; to what others are offering.

All knowledge is a valuable asset. To start I outline what I have trained in and or have acquired knowledge of. Other SiReiki masters will work diligently with me to develop how to use their knowledge to benefit their practice, and make something unique and beautiful.

I've not trained with any of these companies personally, so this is just to point out what options are available. Please do some online searching. Make sure to check if their certification is adequate where you want to practice, as requirements vary. I'm only listing the most affordable training. If the links don't work at the time of reading, I apologise. Always check out my blog for updated information, classes and resource links.

To practice aromatherapy massage, you will need a certification that covers anatomy and physiology, essential oil safety and effects, and massage. You can get a simpler qualification to just use a burner with essential oils that only covers oil composition and safety, but you will not be qualified to apply the oils to a client.

As with Reiki, insurance is a requirement, but is usually very affordable. Don't conduct a session without it!

Distance courses:
https://www.coe-onlinetrainingcourses.com/

Various online courses are available including aromatherapy, A&P, massage and crystals all under £40 each with a discount code. The courses are usually several hundred pounds. This is by far the most affordable option though you will have to check if it meets requirements where you want to practice.

Here is another:

https://www.naturalhealthcourses.com/courses/aromatherapy/?gclid=CjwKEAjw-_e7BRDs97mdpJzXwh0SJABSdUH0zaKyiA1ltPloW_rXtC86T9wwYtzm7ZosfjSfAtNwoRoCG3zw_wcB

£135 self-guided recognised in USA and UK for basic course and extended course £195.

https://www.naturalhealthcourses.com/courses/advanced-aromatherapy/ Total price £330

In person UK:

https://www.gatewayworkshops.co.uk/ a variety of courses, different levels of qualifications.

https://www.gatewayworkshops.co.uk/spiritual_courses/crystal-healing-courses/

A good grounding in crystals for £140 (though I am not sure how it contrasts to other courses only that it is to a suitable standard as my wife have used them previously).

Check your local college financial help may be available. Personally, if the UK qualification is not up to diploma (level 3) qualification, it's not worth the paper it's written on, so please be cautious.

Typical training scenario and Pricing

Not sure where to go, but definitely like what you are reading here? Part of my purpose is to share this knowledge and healing with others. I offer attunements for Usui, with additional opportunities for students to begin SiReiki© once Usui training is complete. Knowing the benefit these programs bring to the world, I am offering a discounted price of 20% for those who are not employed, are chronically ill (mentally, physically or socially), disabled or retired. Discounts of 10% are given to groups of two or more people when booking. Some food and drinks are included in the price if attunement is done in person (all vegan).

Distant teaching will be an integral part of my practice, but this will be distance training with a difference.

Master Practitioner and Teacher are taught as separate levels, though they can be taught at the same time in some cases. Interested students can reach me via email or my social media outlets.

Embracing the Next Level in Your Journey – Understanding and Exploring the Tenets of SiReiki©

To move students into this new territory of understanding, I have translated my approach to distinguish the techniques, timing and commitment needed to achieve each level. The information below is applicable for both in person and distance learning opportunities.

SiReiki© level 1:
SiReiki© level 1 is much like Usui Reiki level 1. It is about the foundations of learning and self-healing. Yes, you're a Usui Master, but let's refocus before we can expand.

Level 1 will enhance your Reiki practice. You will start to utilise other techniques that are optional; first for yourself, but eventually for your clients too.

Level 1 SiReiki© - 1 Day Attunement and technique practice. Expanding on the original Usui Reiki Core with elements such as developed crystal healing, aromatherapy, enhanced grounding and protection, enhanced emotional healing, enhanced distance healing, enhanced breathing and much more.

- Students receive a printed manual containing key information which can also act as a means to document their personal reflections on each activity.
- Each student may learn differently, so I have incorporated 3 case studies based on additional techniques to illustrate them.
- No one learns in a vacuum. Ongoing communication is critical to the journey of learning. I personally integrate online, email, blog support and live chat options into all student programs. You are never alone in this journey.
- Post-education assessment demonstrates comprehension, knowledge retention, and areas for additional review. Students participate in a short recap after the case study review (2 hours) followed by evaluation. Students achieve certification through demonstration of knowledge and skill levels.

*Level 1 requires separate training funded separately (UK standard): (*Level 3) Diploma training in Anatomy & Physiology, Aromatherapy massage and Essential oil training. (It is a legal requirement that you have certification in these areas in order to practice them on clients).

Level 2 SiReiki©:
Level 2 SiReiki© – 1-day attunement and technique process. Students explore further developed techniques designed for professional use.

- More detailed case studies are presented. These 4 case studies explore the next level of achievements for a student to comprehend.
- Building upon the Level 1 training, students will be presented with many developments and enhancements that progress naturally from the prior training.
- Students receive a printed manual containing key information and which can also act a means to document their personal reflections on each activity.
- To maintain communications, students receive full online support.
- Post-education assessment demonstrates comprehension, knowledge retention, and areas for additional review. Students participate in a short recap after the case study review (2 hours) followed by evaluation. Students achieve certification through demonstration of knowledge and skill levels.

Level 3 SiReiki© Master practitioner:
Level 3 SiReiki© - One-and-a-half-day attunement and technique practice.
- Seven holistic SiReiki© case studies bring the student an exceptional view of actualizing established and new skills.
- All techniques are taught to their broadest, most detailed level.
- Post-education assessment demonstrates comprehension, knowledge retention, and areas for additional review. Students participate in a half day recap

followed by evaluation. Students achieve certification through demonstration of knowledge and skill levels.
- Full online support affords continued communication and growth.

It's been a dream, and now it's a reality.
I've always wanted to spread healing to as many people as possible.
I guess I come from a generation of heroes in popular culture that has made me want to be the best "me" there is.

I want more people to heal each other but I know I can't do it alone. Maybe I can inspire others to do their part, and together we can make a difference. There are more light workers on earth now more than ever. The earth is calling and the people are answering in hordes. The earth needs you, the inhabitants need you, and you can make a living using your gifts.

Warriors of light unite in peace and love.

Namaste

Starting out your journey

A journey of a thousand miles starts with a single step so wear some comfortable vegan shoes.

I'm not here to preach or judge. I am not superior to you, and you are not superior to me. We are equal. We are one. We are all connected. I am here to teach and learn. Do you want to go on this journey with me?

In the next Chapter, I'm going to break down the preparation required to learn Reiki into 3 steps.

If you're learning Usui Reiki, this is useful preparation.

If you are a Master and about to embrace SiReiki©, then you might just read on to find that there is more to be learned. If you treat yourself and others with respect leading up to the attunement process, you're going to get more out of it and have less detoxification symptoms. Do your best but don't be too hard on yourself. This is your journey and you don't have to skip to the finish line right away.

Work at your own pace.

Chapter 3

Level with me! I'm interested, but how do I get the best out of my journey?

Photo credit Amanda Clarke

Step One: Educate

So you want to learn to heal yourself and or others? Or maybe you want to be more spiritually active. Great! Reiki is for you!

Do you think Reiki practitioners are special? Are you awake and see the potential in every human being on this planet?

Thoughts control energy. Master your emotions to master your healing potential and master your vitality for life, for your spirit.

Compassion. Empathy. Love. They all overlap but it is the same force... positive emotions.

The more you can look at a client as a fellow earthling that you are connected to and love, even if you have never met them before, the better a Reiki healer you will be, regardless of what system you use.

To develop your compassion, I have extended the Reiki principles and developed training techniques to increase healing potential through unconditional positive regard displaying unconditional love.

Check the blog https://www.sireiki.org for background reading to do at your own pace. Comment with your questions and check back often for responses.

Watch educational documentaries that will help to awaken you such as: Forks Over Knives, That Sugar Film, Food Inc., Cowspiracy, What the Health, Earthlings, Home (viewer discretion advised). Documentaries like these will open your eyes and you might not like what you see. The truth is hard and so is waking up. You can find many of these titles on You Tube or your online streaming provider.

There is a lot more recent stuff out now or coming out soon. The world is opening up its eyes. Welcome to the age of the awaking.

Documentaries like these will help you decipher food programming and help you decide what you should put in your body as fuel. For years I was eating the diet I was born into, not knowing that it deducted from my spiritual path. I guess I was still waking up.
Now that I've been vegan for a while, I can tell you that spirituality, Reiki and veganism are all interlinked.

You may not be ready to embrace your true path yet, but I would hope eventually you would get it. Show your spiritual-self more respect and don't consume anything that came from an animal. I have love and respect for all, but I can never go back to consuming animal products. Since I have done this, my spiritual life has grown along with my health and wellbeing.

Step Two: Prepare

As a preparation for your first attunement, you have to be mindful of what you put into your body. You are what you eat. So five weeks before your attunement, a detoxification process should be started.

Going plant based is the healthiest, most ethical dietary choice. In doing so, you will enhance your Reiki practice. Your Ki flow will be of a higher vibration without the pain of the digested animal in your vessel, affecting you negatively spiritually.

Once you're plant based, going full vegan is easy and definitely will help further increase your vibration. During detoxification, as practical as possible, try to cut down on processed foods and other synthetic foods. Avoid meat, eggs, and dairy, while drinking plenty of filtered water and eating plenty of fruit and veggies, organic if possible.

You don't have to calorie restrict. Eat as much as you feel you need. If you wish to go the "whole hog" and go vegan, I applaud you and thank you for your contribution to this beautiful earth.

Be cautious what chemicals you're exposed to on a daily basis. Fluoride is a nasty little poison. So please check your water supply and use non-fluoride tooth paste. This will help your progression.

If you are on medication, don't stop taking it.
Carry on as normal and if you need to see your doctor for advice.

The preparation for your first attunement is a purification process, so try to avoid drugs and alcohol if possible. If you can't, just do your best.

Reiki principles again ... They are helpful, so try to use them even before you are attuned. This will help the development process.

Later in the book, I have very briefly discussed my own principles in addition to the originals; follow which ever you are in alignment with. Use the blog https://www.sireiki.org . This has many topics to help inspire you, along with other online support such as my Facebook Reiki page.

If you can, try practicing relaxation and meditation techniques. This will help develop your mind, body, and spirit. There are many meditation resources online and local groups that meet regularly. I would recommend visualization as well, as this will help you prepare for Usui Reiki & SiReiki©.

Step Three: Attunements & Knowledge

Attunement:

My doors are open but I might not resonate with you for one reason or another. So I would say if not from me find a master you really connect with emotionally or spiritually. Lineage is important for some but it's all from the same source. So chose the teacher, maybe meet for a chat before you book the attunement and get a feel for them and get a taste for where they are with their Reiki path.

At least three attunements are required for Usui Reiki and 3 or more attunements are required for SiReiki©.

So what is an attunement? It is a permanent opening, aligning and enhancement of your chakras and energy system to be able to channel Reiki life force energy forever.

I would always suggest an in person attunement, but in today's modern world, there is no reason why the process can't be done over live chat if travelling is a problem. I see many teachers offering distant online training with distant attunements. I don't feel as if this provides enough support without live attunements and with chats, you're basically learning from a book.

The way I teach Reiki distantly is the same way I teach it in person, just over live chat and video chat. The attunement is given remotely, live on chat, in the comfort of your own home. There is no difference in time dedicated to your learning. When you learn with me online, it is easier access and convenient.

If you are disabled and have transportation issues, or are an international student, you can still learn in a comfortable, affordable way, without compromising on quality. Let's use technology to bring us closer together, not further apart.

Knowledge:

Usui Reiki was designed to be simple at its starting levels ... Even a cat or dog can be attuned to level 1, and if you have a pet, I would recommend it.

The original system was designed to be very simple, a universal system. Most people can effectively master this system if they embrace it and prepare for spiritual growth and development. SiReiki© is a little more, well complex is not the correct word; it's simply expands from the Usui base. It is designed as a continuation of learning for increased effectiveness with increased client centred practice.

Some additional reading is a must, as is certification. Remember though, certification is not always necessarily required unless you want to utilise some additional skills such as aromatherapy and massage. Some people will find level 1 SiReiki© is enough for them. Others will want to learn all 3 levels. This is your journey. Take it one step at a time.

I will only attune people to master teacher SiReiki© who are dedicated about the path. There is a big shift from level 1 Usui Reiki to Master Teacher SiReiki©. It won't be for everyone, so my advice is just take your time with the journey.

Please note 3- 6 months should pass between each attunement process.

My advice is to start with a single step on the SiReiki© journey and add to your knowledge base when you are ready.

SiReiki© Level 1 background info and reading to expand your journey

Reiki Principles

I have added a few tools in the first manual that I think are essential for spiritual development. The principles will help you live a vital happy life and have successful Reiki practice.

Please use under your own consideration. The below are life recommendations which are spiritual in nature. No religious belief is required; of course Reiki should not and will not insult or conflict with any true religious belief either.

Just for today: (as our original master stated) follow the principles

Today is now so be in the now, for that is the center of peace of yourself.

Therefore, to incorporate mindfulness, SiReiki© states just for now, this moment, apply the principles and you will live in a state of much blessings.

The present moment *will never come again...*
Try not to do something you will regret, as this will weigh you down and make your journey more difficult than it needs to be.

Try to follow the principles. I guarantee if you stick to them, you will be a better healer and a happier person. :D

If you slip up, try again tomorrow or in the next now... Breathe! Feel your body centre itself in love and be mindful...
Then you will appreciate the beauty around and within you.

<u>Photo credit Amanda Clarke</u>

Usui Reiki Principles:

Just for today...

I will not anger.

I will not worry.

I will be grateful for life's many blessings.

I will do my work with honesty and integrity.

I will be kind to all living things.

I will find joy in life.

In keeping with the original principles, SiReiki© principles are simplistic in nature and will not alienate any religious viewpoints. Despite their simple nature, mastery is very much linked with a healthier Reiki practice and spiritual life. Please don't overlook them and try to stick to them every day. One day at a time. I introduce spiritual practice in my first manual "SiReiki© Becoming". For now, read on to get a taste for it.

SiReiki© Principles:
In this moment: Be Thankful
If you wish to be abundant, you must appreciate what you have first. Life is a gift with many presents. The universe, through the law of attraction, will bring more to you if you are grateful. Furthermore, you are more likely to treat your fellow earthling with respect and generosity, generating good Karma and positivity in the world.

In this moment: Spread happiness.
We all need happiness! Spread it and make it fun! Spread it however you like as long as you have respect and don't hurt yourself or others. If you can't be happy, try to be positive. Remember, we all have "bad days", but how we treat others has a chain effect. So if you have to share something with someone, why not a smile? Go on, you can manage a grin just for a second.

In this moment: Do not direct anger at yourself or others. Be Peaceful.
Anger is mostly a destructive force unless it serves the greater good in inspiring rapid action. Most of the time, getting angry is an overstretch of how you really feel. This is because we feel anger as a physical chemical reaction. It must be countered. If you don't release it, anger adds up and the person you're getting angry at surely does not deserve your full frustration. We also get angry over silly things for the same reason, and getting aggressive over something silly is a bit daft! Take a second to breathe. Namaste.

In this moment: Love yourself and everyone else.
All life comes from the Creator. Love all earthlings, as they are your family. Namaste. It is not easy to feel love for everyone, but it is a beautiful thing. Simple unified love of being an earthling, is something that draws us together. There is no need to be ashamed. Unconditional love is a beautiful thing.

In this moment: Respect your teachers and elders. Be respectful.
Life is for learning. That is why we are here. Honor all who teach you valuable lessons, however they are presented. We never stop learning. Be nice to those who have taught you something. Some lessons come from those who did it in a not so nice way. We are on this earth to evolve, so respect all mediums of learning.

In this moment: Be honest.
Honesty is a rare thing but there is innocence in it and it is needed for trust. I sometimes say the truth without tact. Try not to follow my example and if you need to, take a breath and rethink. Words are like glass; they can hurt you if you're not careful with them. Being honest is being congruent and with that comes a freedom of truth. There are only a few exceptions why you should lie, but it should be your last option and only if it serves the greater good, but please never lie to yourself.

In this moment: Be responsible for yourself, your Earth, and its inhabitants.
We need this Earth to survive so we better take good care of it. It's not rocket science, just leave it a better place than you found it, any way you can. People learn from other's mistakes and achievements. Be the inspiration! Go vegan!

Mother earth is a beautiful planet. Let's not make too much of a mess of it. Please, before it is too late, be responsible for your impact on this planet and the earthlings on it. You don't have to be an eco-warrior, but you can make a huge difference in your day to day life.

Changing your diet may not be high on your priorities right now, but it could make all the difference. It's not the answer to everything, but it's the biggest piece of the puzzle for the future. Go vegan. By going vegan, we can feed more, live longer and have healthier lives.
We will have less negative impact on the Earth and its earthlings. By doing that one simple thing, you will be a more effective healer and have a more peaceful soul.

For some, the focus is mostly on the healing aspects and that's fine. I got into Reiki and veganism firstly to encourage healing. When you factor ethical issues of what can be done to reduce suffering in animals and humans alike, that is what drives and keeps you vegan; and keeps you using your Reiki. It's the human and animal aspect that deepens the meaning. With Reiki, we realise we are all the same, we can all reach out and help each other as a global web of healing. With veganism, we understand the wrongs must be undone. We must be kind to this earth and all its inhabitants.

The world is being raped in the name of profit. Don't get angry just take action. What you put on your plate, with your money, shapes the world as well and makes up your very cells.

I could recommend some compassion for yourself and your earthling brothers and sisters by being mindful of what you consume.
Change often comes slowly but when the scale tips, you will feel it and know the weight has shifted.

For me, the Christian paraphrased example of, "and behold God has planted every seed to provide you all you need to sustain and heal yourself, the animals will be your companions, together the world is yours."

Photo credit Amanda Clarke

If you ever wished the world was a better place, make it this way.

The less we negatively impact ourselves and our planet and its inhabitants the better.

As a social note, I would like to apologise for some vegans. We are a passionate group who are not ok with animal abuse, period. We can get a reputation as being, you know, "that vegan". I am by no means a perfect vegan. But being vegan does not mean you have never made a mistake. It's simply a statement of intent, a compass that will always direct me.

We respect you even if you don't follow our lifestyle, but sometimes we come off as superior (we're not) as we know it's a better way to live for all. We are not perfect. Sometimes we can be harsh on our fellow vegans and non-vegans for not being the very best example. Non-vegans can try to poke fun at vegans because it takes attention away from the harm they are inflicting. It's not their fault. Repeated lies and propaganda given by the food industry are powerful! We have all been programed to be good customers. We try as vegans to open your eyes, but are judged and ridiculed as we try to shake your foundation. This causes resentment and frustration.

Believe us. We are right in our respect for all earthlings and the Earth. Going vegan is the way forward. This can make us very vocal about the subject and not everyone appreciates this. The media tries to show veganism as extreme. This is far from the truth. The cutting edge of medicine, socialists and freethinkers alike agree vegan is the way. It's a new way of thinking and could completely change the nature of global health and wellbeing for all.

So for your fellow earthlings and your Mother Earth, try to go vegan, even if it's just one meal at a time.

I mean no disrespect to any non-vegan Reiki masters it is your path walk it however you are guided.

I'm not going to focus on why you should change your lifestyle I'm going to tell you the good things that will happen if you do.

For some this could be the start of a new journey. Others might keep their old habits but just be open to change and even a modest improvement is good for the planet and its inhabitants.

On a vegan diet we will have more than enough food to feed every human on the entire planet and then some! Providing a healthy diet for all, in an affordable way.

Wild animals don't really need much input from humans but they do need some where to live. If more of us went vegan, we can dramatically reduce deforestation and stop the mass extinction of animals.

Without so much land being used for animal agriculture, we can make the earth lush again. Giving plenty of space for all. While seriously reducing dangerous emissions that affect our climate and helping to reduce environmental contamination and waste of water.

You can make such a positive impact on the earth just by making a few changes. So ask yourself is it worth a try? You can save over 100 farmed animals every year, save so much precious water, stop wild animals going extinct, be healthier, live longer and repair our damaged earth by going vegan.

Remember I'm not judging you, I just want to plant the seeds of change. If you want support on your journey reach out to me.

We can take this a step at a time and see how you feel. For the purpose of the attunement, I want you to try a 5-week plan prior to your attunement. If you chose not to take my advice, it's ok maybe it's not your time yet; but at least read what I propose. The purer you are the better the process of the attunement will be with less detoxification.

Just a note but if you don't follow my recommendations but have still made an effort for you, then I would be happy to book your attunement. Read on and give it a try I'll see you on attunement day.

I want you to remember that doing your best is enough. If you have started to educate yourself on veganism, then making a few changes will come naturally. But if you're not ready for the full change yet, just do your best.

The plan that follows is just a suggestion. You can follow it as closely as you would like.

You don't have to be vegan to practice Reiki but it is a personal recommendation to get the most out of your path.

In the next chapter I outline a brief plan of how to truly align your diet to a spiritual lifestyle, for all our good, by going vegan. For the good of your earthlings, the planet, and for your Reiki and spiritual practice, try it out and see if it's for you.

The following plan can be extended. More gradual detoxification can be done by simply spending 2 weeks on the one-week plan.

If this does not apply to the extent you wish to engage in, then use this to the extent that it does. Do your best. If you have watched the recommended documentaries, then this will be an easier journey. If you have not, check out a few. You have nothing to lose by trying this, but potentially a lot to gain.

You don't have to be an activist with a placard! You can be an activist with your debit card.

If you feel you want extra help, chat to me online or ask a question at my blog *https://www.sireiki.org/* Or my small but perfectly formed Reiki Group
https://www.facebook.com/groups/299404700398325/
https://www.instagram.com/sireiki/

If you think eating meat
is a personal choice,
you are forgetting
someone.
Male chicks are a byproduct
of the egg industry. They are
ground up alive within one
day of hatching.
*Go Vegan

Chapter 4
You want me to eat F*****G twigs!?

Photo credit and cook Amanda Clarke

Diet Preparation Week One

Okay, I won't do your research for you, that's your journey, but I'll share a few snippets of my viewpoint based on the research I have come across and facts I am aware of.

Now I write to you this morning turning over a new leaf. This chapter originally contained a somewhat grim description of what happens to you and the animals when you consume animal products. I wanted to open eyes and educate but I lost the message in the process.

For this I am sorry. Yes, it was factual and helpful but the message was all wrong.
It's not about shame, or blame, or guilt these are low vibrationary emotions. We don't need them we want instead to focus on healthy feelings such as self-respect and unconditional love and empathy for all.

So I am rewriting this chapter to reflect the message of SiReiki.

A gentle note on milk

Most people are lactose intolerant by nature because our milk is that of our mothers, not a calf's mother. Have you ever looked at a food label and asked milk??? Why do we need milk in this recipe? Or guess the extra ingredient as we produce too much of it... drum roll ... yep cheese.

Food manufacturers place milk in most products because it is more addictive. The more addictive something is, the more you will want to buy it and the more regularly you will you decide to put it in your basket. It is that simple people.

But doesn't milk contain calcium for strong bones right? Yes, milk contains calcium but so do plants while not being damaging to the body like dairy is. One of the ways dairy is damaging is due to the fact that dairy leaches calcium from the bones in response to making the body more acidic.

Cases of fractures due to low bone density have been categorically linked to dairy consuming populous; With World Health Organization (WHO) reporting prevalence of such in a high dairy consuming populous that is far elevated from populous with low diary consumption.

Plant sources of calcium show greater bone health with less instances of disease or fractures. Breastmilk is natural but each to their own. It is designed to make an infant grow strong and healthy.

When we mature, we can consume plant milk. Plant milk is nutritious and easily absorbed, with no suffering or death of an animal is needed.

Soya has received mixed attention with the usual dairy backed research trying to document that it is unhealthy. Non-corrupted research of non GM soya shows many health benefits. But soya can be adulterated too, so just bear in mind added sugar, etc. Companies like to turn healthy foods and make them more addictive through lots of sugar. So bear in mind not all brands are the same, and each brand now has lots of variants as they try and take over the dairy market.

I think farmers are hardworking and deserve a living, but not at the expense of animals. Slaughterhouses however have no place in ethical society. It's up to you, the consumer, to shut them down by taking those items out of your cart. You might not see it, but if you buy it, the blood is on your hands. Dairy farmers, please manufacture and sell plant milk and grow organic fruit and vegetables. It is the way forward. It is kinder to all and there is plenty of profit in non GM plant milk and healthy fruit and vegetables.

Without dairy, food tastes better and you will naturally crave healthier nutritious foods. This is because diary lines the taste buds. When you eliminate it, food tastes sharper and cleaner so you will be drawn to more natural tasting food.

Common sense would also tell us with regard to our antibiotics crisis, that we should lower/avoid foods that lower the effectiveness of antibiotics, when we really need it. This useful medicine becomes less effective by flooding our bodies with dairy laced with antibiotics. When you consider that dairy is an item that is in most foods it's easy to understand why we have a problem. The industry does not care about your wellbeing or the animal's wellbeing. In the age of factory farming, cash is king.

Weekly affirmation:
Remember you are not a baby cow, period! (Yes I am cheesy!).
Start the week: Monday, no milk... Wednesday, no cheese, Thursday no eggs, over the weekend look in your freezer, fridge and cupboard and start to eat up your food with added milk, eggs and cheese.

A lot of changes for the start, but believe me, this is the best way if you want a quick change. You're going to need to look for vegan options to discover alternatives that you like. Enjoy the journey. Peace.

It's not the easiest step, but be aware there is a vegan alternative for every animal product. Try some research and reading.

I would recommend non GM soy milk for a good all-rounder; though some brands you'll have to heat before adding to coffee (use filter coffee, not instant). Formable oat milk is excellent in coffee, but non-forming hemp, almond milk, and rice milk are also delicious. Coconut milk is perfect for smoothies, but you can use any milk alternative you choose in a smoothie. There is so many types of milk, have fun seeing what you enjoy. Vegetable milk is an excellent way to get in extra nutrition that won't hurt your health. Try to avoid using sweetened variants too regularly. I use them in all ways that I used to use cow's milk. Play around and see what works for you.

Milk:
Most plant milk will be fine with tea but some reacts to coffee especially instant coffee. I use a cafeteria and warm up my milk to avoid this (you don't have to warm the milk it just helps). Some brands of fresh coffee can still react, but most don't. A bit of trial and error is needed. From my perspective, soya original is best in tea and is a good base for cooking. It can be used in filter coffee, but look out for curdling it's down to the brand of coffee and soy.

Not all plain soy is made equal, some will even be stable enough for instant coffee, unfortunately quality and price go hand in hand. Another tip if you're mixing soy with instant coffee is to make sure the coffee is well stirred and cooled a little before you add the soy and mix well as you pour. Don't just add a drop of soy, put in a good glug this will help it mix. There you go no curdle. It's annoying when that happens, some makes of coffee however will always curdle soy, so experiment.

Chocolate and vanilla soy is excellent in coffee and usually won't curdle. It is also amazing in hot chocolate and smoothies, as is almond milk.

Best way to enjoy almond milk is to make your own as the quality varies much between brands; it's not too difficult to make. If not, try a few good brands and see what works for you.

Hemp can be used in many ways and is generally more stable than normal soy. It is packed full of goodies and tastes great in coffee. Oat formable and non-formable is very healthy, gives a gentler taste to other varieties. Cashew and hazelnut have less application. I use them more as a treat for something different; but those who love it, love it!

Coconut is your smoothie king or very refreshing on its own and makes a good coffee. So look for taste, colour, and stability. Can you make a brew with it, health properties?

When you find a few that work for you, you can do some research about it. It will give you a better appreciation for it.

Plant milk is a lot healthier than animal milk, just be aware of sugar content and GM soya. I have some sweetened as a treat and reduce added sugar to compensate. Oh no GM soy you say! Well don't worry most GM soy is used to feed to livestock, though labelling is not yet mandatory so shop mindfully.

One advantage to switching from dairy is fat content. Fat content will be lower especially saturated fat. In addition to this, there is no cholesterol or animal hormones or pus. Best of all – no cruelty. Be aware of bogus research, articles published by the dairy industry are sponsored and you will come across them.

The dairy industry days are numbered but they are not going down without a fight. So put your bullshit glasses on and find good research.

Cheese:
Vegan cheese is a healthier alternative and new options are coming out all the time. So experiment and see what you like.

Vegan cheese has come a big way over the past few years. It is far healthier and some brands taste great. Note it does not always melt the same way as traditional cheese, experiment.

The taste is different to traditional cheese as the ingredients are very different, with some being very similar and others something new entirely. Love it, hate it, or tolerate it, vegan cheese is an ethical choice that is entirely made with plants, not cardboard! A bit of trial and error is required to find what works for you. If the first thing you try is not for you, try something else. There are a lot of variants within the brands.

My favourite use of vegan cheese is to melt with some soya milk and make a rich cheese dressing. Simply warm your soya or use boiling water and add your chosen cheese until it's at your chosen consistency, adding more soya as required, while gently heating. I usually make a mixture of hard, spreadable, nutritional yeast and vegan butter with some salt and pepper.

When you convert from traditional dairy to non-dairy alternatives, you need to be kind to yourself. It is going to take some adjustment and educating yourself is key. You may have given it no thought but you have been addicted to dairy. The food industry has encouraged this since you were a child by adding it to most food groups, while advertising heavily to us while we are most vulnerable. Vegan cheese is not addictive chemically in any way. It is much kinder on the body as it's made from plants. You will likely still enjoy the taste and some of it is close to the original. That being said, it's not the same and you will have to see what you like and what you do not. You will only replace the taste, not the addiction. Used in moderation, you can help to offset your preventable disease risks while doing your bit for the animals and the environment.

Ok, time to shop, so think taste, melt-ability, spread-ability, affordability and health. P.S. Don't forget about nutritional yeast. It is healthy and adds extra flavour to your food.

Ok, I know I have given you a lot to do this week, but as an extra task to help you adapt, I would like for you to find a coffee shop that offers a vegan cappuccino or latte. If they have vegan cake, all the better.

Photo credit Amanda Clarke

Week two

Ok, so you have cut out a lot of nasties already and tried some new tasty things. Maybe you did not love it all, but just eat what appeals to you. This may change as your body adjusts, so don't be surprised if that happens.

This week we are going to eliminate more animal products. So it's all about the added ingredients, the ones that you won't always think that are in your food on first thought. Milk, cheese, eggs and other animal products are added to a lot of food so you have to start looking at the labels. Look out for the **bold** wording and if it's not in the main ingredient list, you're good to go. Most often, the food is made in a factory that does use milk etc. So they put, "may contain", just to cover their back in case of cross contamination.

So here is the plan, last week you started to eat up your added dairy by Wednesday. I want you to have finished eating up and start with no eggs, cheese, and animal milk. It's ok if you slip up, but now it is all about breaking out of your food addiction and conditioning.

Keep it up, it is hard at first but it becomes easier. I promise! You just need to get proactive about what you eat. By Thursday, I want you to have put your money where your mouth is and buy more vegan foods.

Weekly affirmation:
Animals are friends, not food. Leave them alone, don't be rude.

Photo credit Amanda Clarke

Vegan Butter:
Okay, time to try vegan butter generally without the animal products. Vegan butter is a heather alternative. Some variants are better for you than others, but right now I just want you to find one that you like. Think taste, spread-ability, oil content, and health properties. I use coconut, soya and olive oil spreads, with no dairy, that don't depend too much on high oil content. Plant butter can be a healthier option, but it's a new art so some is healthier than others. Avoid ones with large amounts of oil content in excess, it's not healthy.

Ice Cream:
Vegan ice cream is delicious and surprisingly it's a healthier alternative. It is not a health food however, and too much is still bad for you. If you want to go the healthy route, homemade ice cream is the best thing to do. For now, try some pre-made, no suffering and slightly-better-for-you-than-the-supermarket variety...enjoy ;)

Eggs:
Tofu scramble is my egg substitute of choice, but there are a few other options out there. There are a lot of different tofu so try a few. Unless you plan to pre-season it I would go for one that's already seasoned. If you need a natural replacement for egg in baking, add 1 ripe banana per egg, or one tablespoon of ground and soaked chia seed paste.

Chocolate:
Dairy free is always healthier and we all need a little chocolate in our lives. Baking can be fun and simple with a few adjustments, so keep an eye out for some simple recipes you want to try. That will come later. For now, look for dairy free chocolate, accidently vegan chocolate! This happens a lot with higher coco bars, but that's not everyone's cup of tea. For an affordable option, I would go for a vegan 70% coco chocolate. You can find it widespread. Check that label and find one you like.

Chocolate that's labelled vegan will cost extra, usually but they will use tasty ingredients such as plant milk and fats to replace the cow's milk. So you don't have to go with the dark option. Nero Coffee Shop has a vegan chocolate option. It's not labelled vegan but it is, so maybe pop in and sample some. Vego is my favourite bar, but some high end bars are a bit on the expensive side. Vegan brownies can be made quite affordably! My wife makes them. Delicious!

One thing you will find is once you cut out the dairy chocolate, you will tend to have a healthier relationship with chocolate, as you are cutting out the harmful and addictive ingredients. Don't be surprised if you eat less chocolate less often, which if you used to have a strong addiction to chocolate was because of the dairy. This could help to keep you at optimum weight. Think quality over quantity, but if you get high quality, then until vegan chocolate hits the masses, be prepared to pay for it. If you find one that you really like, you can save some money by buying it online, a few at a time.

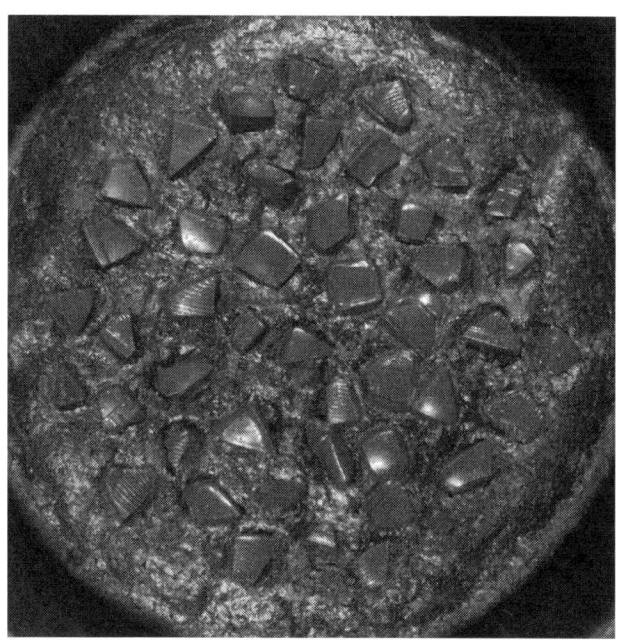

Photo credit Amanda Clarke

Week Three:

Congratulations, you made it! Well done! You ok? The rest is easier I promise.

Weekly affirmation:
Where do I get my protein from? Go ask that gorilla!

If you want to be as strong as an elephant or gorilla or rhino, eat your veggies.

This week we are going to focus on reducing meat intake and for good reason. So I am trying very hard not to go on a rant why meat is bad for you and the environment.
Yes, a human can get some basic nutrition from meat but we have a hard time digesting it. If you think I'm wrong, go raw eating a fresh kill and see how good you feel lol. Furthermore, it's not what your body wants and for the most part, it's second hand nutrition from the source plants.

Carnivores all have a very distinctive physiology. One common aspect we do know is that all carnivores have a short digestive tract, in order to digest the flesh quickly before it decomposes. Human beings have a very long digestive tract, because we are not designed to use flesh as our primary source of food. We are designed to be plant based. If you want health and a long life, that's the way you need to go. By all means, do your own research. This has to come from you, but the best doctors and physicians are plant based.

Yes, sorry I did rant a bit I'm sorry but I have to get the message out their people.

Keep up the good work. Celebrate what you have done so far you have earnt it.

Hang in there! You can do this... :)

Did you slip up, or are you dedicated? Either way, just keep trying! Eventually you will prefer things this way and your body will thank you for it. If not, you can always go back to how you did things before. What do you have to lose?

Photo credit Amanda Clarke

This week I want you to halve your meat intake while eating more vegetables. For extra homework find somewhere to eat a vegan meal with friend or a loved one.

As far as what's healthy and what tastes good, you will just have to let your taste buds do the talking. Organic veg can be very different, it looks and tastes better, if not a wee bit scruffier, and yes, sadly more expensive; but health treatment costs more than prevention.

No problem, ok earthlings? You can do this.

If you see beauty in an animal that you don't eat; then you must also recognise the same beauty it in all living beings that you have eaten. All beings are made of the same energy, they all want to live and deserve at the very least respect for their right to exist for their own purposes.

End the holocaust. End the slavery

Photo credit Amanda Clarke

Photo credit Amanda Clarke

Photo credit Amanda Clarke

Photo credit Amanda Clarke

I'm so proud of you for doing this!

Namaste

Use the blogs for support and check out some vegan Facebook groups for great ideas and support.

Week Four
Weekly affirmation: "I don't need meat not even as a treat."

Ok guys you're doing great let's keep it going.

I want you to avoid meat all together. Yes, I know it's a big step, but you won't lose out as you can try some meat replacements.

There are a lot of vegetarian meat replacements on the market. They like to still keep you addicted. An addicted customer is a regular customer. So before you buy, read the ingredients list, check for sneaky added **milk**, **cheese**, and **egg** in alternatives (look for the vegan label). If it says this may contain traces, that's okay. They may be made in a factory that uses those ingredients. So, just replacements only: No egg, milk, cheese, meat …

As far as meat alternatives go, avoid too many chemicals. Keep it simple, the closer the veg is to their original state the greater likelihood it is healthier for you. Try some seitan its very tasty and far healthier for you than meat.

When compared to processed meat, there is no contrast. Veg based products win every time, but a diet should never depend too much on large amounts of processed food. So as a rule of thumb, treat processed vegetables as a small portion of your daily allowance and you can't go too wrong.

Don't worry about getting it perfect straight away. Your likes and dislikes will naturally change, and this is a big change for the better if you have eliminated your animal products.

Week five
Weekly affirmation: "My body is my vessel I will not settle."

You're nearly there! You have eliminated a lot of bad stuff from your diet. Now it's time to increase the good stuff!

Water:
Drink plenty of water (purified non chlorine). Cut down on caffeine and alcohol, just try a bit, a relative improvement would suffice. If you can't manage now, try at a later time. Increase herbal tea intake. Non-caffeinated drinks are a good way to hydrate and they have other subtle benefits.

Vegetables:

Increase the amount of fruit and vegetables you eat. Perhaps try one or two you have not yet. When you get the hang of it, try to eat some raw veggies if possible. Overcooking vegetables kills nutrients, but one step at a time.

Photo credit Amanda Clarke

Smoothies & Juices

A smoothie and or a juice a day will boost your vitamin and calorie intake and help you regain your energy levels. Avoid sugary milk if possible. Instead, add a little maple syrup. It is nature's sweetener and one of the gentlest on your body. There are many supplemental ingredients you can add to your smoothies such as maca powder or hemp, soft greens are always good too, such as spinach. Do some research and feed yourself some superfood. Also remember to balance fruit and vegetables when you juice to get the correct nutrients and always add with a majority of vegetables to the balance. Veggies such as kale, spinach, cucumber, and carrot can be added to fruit to give you a nutritious juice. Play around and see what works for you.

Photo credit Amanda Clarke

Tips for the future
When you feel you have gotten the hang of plant based, try to not to go too mad on processed food. I know I just got you eating them as a replacement, but a balanced vegan diet should not be dominant on processed food. They should be a small part only that you can eliminate if you so choose to. It is up to you. Don't worry though, even the junk vegan food is a healthier choice. It's just best to keep in mind that you can always make your meals heathier later.

If you slip up its ok people, the worst thing to do is to be too harsh if you're doing your best that's great.

B12 or B vitamin complex:
Most people are actually low in B12, that includes people who eat meat. You may see taking a supplement as unnatural but it's not when you consider cattle are given B12 supplements. Most are no longer getting it naturally from source the Earth. Therefore, large doses of supplements are given on top of the other unnatural elements added to meat.

As we don't eat a lot of dirt nowadays, a B12 supplement is a necessary requirement for all unless, it's been added to your food. If you eat organic vegetables, you can leave a trace of earth on your vegetables to get the B12 naturally. It is always an option, but you don't have to do that to be vegan. Don't worry! Many foods are fortified in B12 such as plant milk and nutritional yeast. I would, however, always recommend a supplement just so it's covered. I would recommend one to anyone, as low levels of B12 are bad for you. You don't have to take big dosages but you need it. If you are worried, get your bloodwork done and see if your diet is enough.

Please remember to be gentle on yourself! You have done well even if you slipped up!

Please see how well you have done.

*Every moment brings an opportunity to follow a healthy lifestyle.
Instead of being a hater to yourself or others, just do your best and hope others follow your example.*

Chapter 5
Ohmmmm, a start to your learning.

Last, but definitely not least.

To create your success, you must visualise it.

To develop your vessel, you must exercise it.

To get the best out of your life you must do the prep work.

To prepare for the methods of Usui Reiki and to a greater extent SiReiki©, you must practice **meditation**, especially with a visualisation element.

You may have learned a Reiki meditation from your original Usui Reiki system. If so use that or complete a Reiki meditation, I go on to describe.

The exact meditation techniques vary with lineage, but it's the element of visualisation of energy that is vitally important. Actively seeing the energy cast and move, will prepare you for SiReiki© techniques.

Here is a simplified Reiki meditation that you can start of your journey with.
This meditation technique can be adapted for a busy schedule or lengthened to really give yourself some tender love and care. This technique is adaptable based on your belief and preference and can be done or adapted to any level of healer.

SiReiki start your day routine

Turn your phone onto silent and put on some relaxing music on a low volume.

Make sure you have put the symbols into the room or if you're yet to be attune, ask for the room to be protected in light. If you have a grid for the room charge and program it now.

Sit with your hands on your legs or your heart centre and close your eyes.

If you have not already ground yourself by imagining a cord attached to your feet, earthing deep into our mother earth, restoring any negative energy back into light. If it's appropriate take of your shoes and socks.

Next, center on your breathing the first step is not to change your breathing just being aware of it is enough.

Is your breath relaxed? Is it full or shallow? How would you like your breathing to be?

Just sit for a moment and just breathe as comes natural. Slow your thoughts, quiet your mind and relax.

If you are attuned, now is the time to get an energy flow going. Cast the Reiki symbols in front of you one at a time. Firstly, just picture the symbol in front of you while holding the image of it in your mind. Say the name of the symbol 3 times, I usually do this silently.

Next, see the symbol move into your hands while saying the name of the symbol 3 times, and tapping the symbol into your hands. Then hold the image of the symbol and see it travel up your front and down your back; saying the name of the symbol 3 times. Imagine and feel a wave of energy flowing with the symbol into your energy pathways clearing blockages as it travels; with any negative energy returning to the mother earth through your grounded pathway to be turned back into light.

Follow this process for all symbols if you are already attuned.

If not, ask for love and light to flow and imagine beautiful white light traveling through your meridians, up your front and down your back.

Next, imagine all chakras radiating a bright beautiful white light and extend this light into a sphere or egg shape around you. Visualise the energy flowing into a dense protection field. Ask or affirm that only love and light penetrate the protection field. Lastly, ask or affirm that the protection remains for 24 hours or longer. You can play around with colours as this will affect the frequency of your energy field I personally recommend white or purple but other vibrations could work equally well.

If you desire, you may extend the meditation with a visualisation element. On attunement day there are many forms of visualisation that may be utilised such as angel, guide, or loved one meditation. This can incorporate a mindfulness breathing technique to continue to quiet the mind, the choice is yours.

To begin, if you have never done this before, simply clear your mind, focus on your breathing and when you're ready see yourself walking through a door of light and into a beautiful beach scene.

Feel the gentle breeze, the warm sun, listen to the relaxing sounds, smell the ocean and rest. You can explore or simply lay on the beach. When you are ready, see yourself entering a door of light and become grounded back into your body.

How is your breathing now? Do you feel more relaxed and at peace?

To conclude the meditation, you have options depending on how much time you have available and what your personal preference is. You can affirm intentions to set up your vibration and/or pray to whoever you pray to (we can develop this on attunement day).

I usually pray first, then affirm that the things I am asking for will manifest in divine timing.

To finish, give thanks for Reiki and the things you are grateful for and seal in the energy.

This technique will help with many things even in its simplified shorter version. The full routine is how I start my day and believe me, it really helps to set the day up.

The routine assists to develop skills, like being more present in the moment, being more centered, being more calm and organized in your own thoughts. Not only this, but now your energy field is well and truly programed. You're grounded and protected in the vortex of your greater good. Now you're set for the day.

Learn the basics now and when it's time for your SiReiki attunement we will develop it further together.

If you follow the guidance that I have set out in this book, I believe you will be working more closely with the Reiki energy than ever before. Even if you're not attune yet do the preparation routine every morning (or as often as you like) and you're going to see the results.

Open your mind to what is possible and you will change what is.

In essence, you can use your imagination to focus the Reiki energy; just as practitioners use symbols. Instead of focusing on the meaning behind a symbol, you become more active with the process, and visualise what is happening with the energy. The trick with this is to be very relaxed but highly focused. Emotions are the key here, especially ones of pure love and empathy. It is true that if you go against the will of the greater good nothing will happen. That is why people relax into the session. What some don't understand is what can be achieved when you join your will to what the greater good wants.

Don't worry about mastery or trouble yourself with worry over how it will be done. Just start small and work from your base.

When you visualise your desire in alignment to the Reiki energy, more can be achieved in a shorter amount of time for a greater number of people.
I hope you join me on my Reiki journey I look forward to working with you all so that you get what you would like out of Reiki.

One step at a time.
Practice with meditation so that your mind and thinking is prepared, enhancing your Reiki practice. Helping you to be in a perfect state of alignment to the Reiki energy.

Thank you my friends for reading. I do hope you have enjoyed the first steps of our journey together.

Namaste love and light,
Simon

I'll see you down the road! Look out for my next book <u>SiReiki© Becoming</u>. It's an instruction guide to accompany your attunement for level 1 SiReiki©; or an interesting read that sparks an interest. It's your choice.

       I will be releasing it soon.

Simon Clarke's Social Media

Website:
https://www.sireiki.org

Facebook Group:

Reiki Brothers and Sisters of love and light <3
https://www.facebook.com/groups/299404700398325/

Instagram:
@Sireiki
https://www.instagram.com/sireiki